Mandala
Abstract Coloring Books

Copyright: Published in the United States by Karen Sanderson
Published January 2017
ISBN-13: 978-1542678971
ISBN-10: 1542678978

All rights reserved. No part of this publication may be reproduced, stored in retrieval system, copied in any form or by any means, electronic, mechanical, photocopying, recording or otherwise transmitted without written permission from the publisher. Please do not participate in or encourage piracy of this material in any way. You must not circulate this book in any format. Karen Sanderson *does not control or direct users' actions and is not responsible for the information or content shared, harm and/or actions of the book readers.*

Thank you

www.ingramcontent.com/pod-product-compliance
Lightning Source LLC
Chambersburg PA
CBHW060014210526
45170CB00018B/2845